TROODON

A Buddy Book
by
Christy Devillier

ABDO
Publishing Company

VISIT US AT

www.abdopub.com

Published by ABDO Publishing Company, 4940 Viking Drive, Edina, Minnesota 55435. Copyright © 2004 by Abdo Consulting Group, Inc. International copyrights reserved in all countries. No part of this book may be reproduced in any form without written permission from the publisher.

Printed in the United States.

Edited by: Michael P. Goecke
Contributing Editor: Matt Ray
Graphic Design: Denise Esner, Maria Hosley
Image Research: Deborah Coldiron
Illustrations: Deborah Coldiron, Denise Esner, Maria Hosley
Photographs: Corel

Library of Congress Cataloging-in-Publication Data

Devillier, Christy, 1971-
    Troodon/Christy Devillier.
        p. cm.
    Includes index.
    Summary: Describes the physical characteristics, habitat, and behavior of a dinosaur with a small body but very large brain.
    ISBN 1-59197-541-7
    1. Troodon—Juvenile literature. [1. Troodon. 2. Dinosaurs.] I. Title.

QE862.S3D49 2004
567.912—dc22

2003057817

TABLE OF CONTENTS

WHAT WERE THEY?

The Troodon may have been one of the smartest dinosaurs. It had a big brain for its body size.

The Troodon lived during the late Cretaceous period. This time period began about 144 million years ago.

Troodon
TRUE-oh-don

The Troodon was not a huge dinosaur. It may have weighed about 100 pounds (45 kg). That is as heavy as a cheetah.

The Troodon was about seven feet (two m) long. It had long legs and a long tail.

The Troodon was about as heavy as a cheetah.

5

HOW DID THEY MOVE?

Many scientists believe the Troodon was a fast runner. It ran on its two back legs.

The Troodon had long arms and legs. It had three toes on each foot. Each toe had a sharp claw.

The Troodon had clawed feet.

The Troodon could grab with its hands. It had three fingers on each hand. Each finger had a sharp claw.

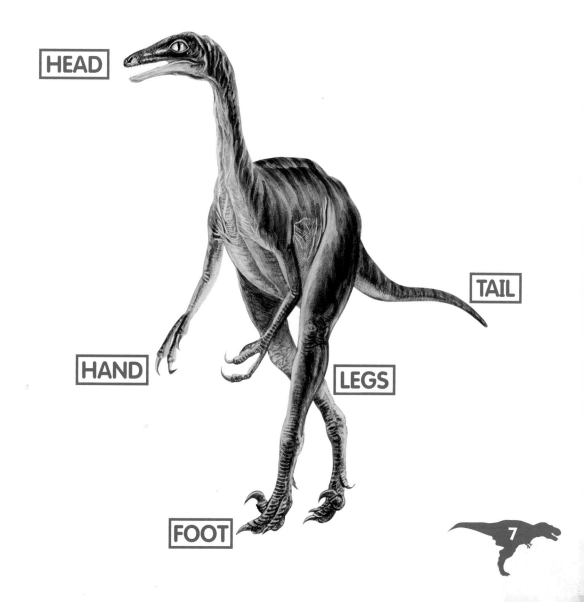

HEAD

TAIL

HAND

LEGS

FOOT

7

WHY WERE THEY SPECIAL?

The Troodon had a special claw on its second toe. This claw was bigger than the other claws. Some scientists called it the "killing claw." The Troodon probably killed prey with its killing claws.

The Troodon may have eaten other dinosaur eggs.

9

WHERE DID THEY LIVE?

The Troodon lived in North America. It lived on land that is now Canada and the United States.

The world was different during the Cretaceous period. The weather was tropical. Forests covered the land. The forests were full of evergreens, palms, and flowering plants.

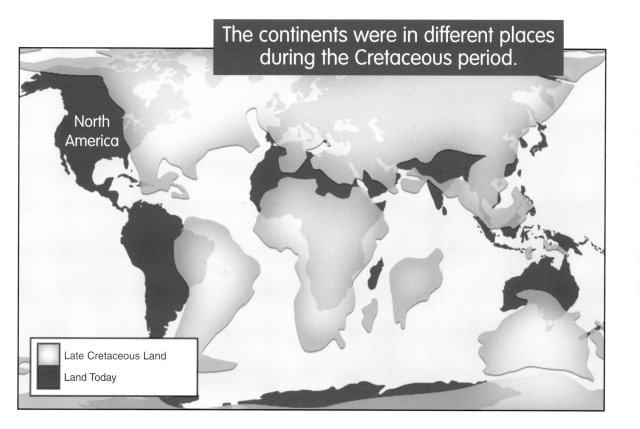

The continents were in different places during the Cretaceous period.

North America

Late Cretaceous Land

Land Today

The Troodon lived among other dinosaurs. It may have lived near the Ankylosaurus. The Ankylosaurus was a plant-eating dinosaur. Hard plates covered its body. The Ankylosaurus also had a club tail.

Hard plates covered the Ankylosaurus.

The Ankylosaurus had a special club tail.

13

The Troodon was a carnivore. Carnivores eat meat. The Troodon hunted other animals. It killed prey with its sharp claws and teeth.

The Troodon's sharp claws helped it kill prey.

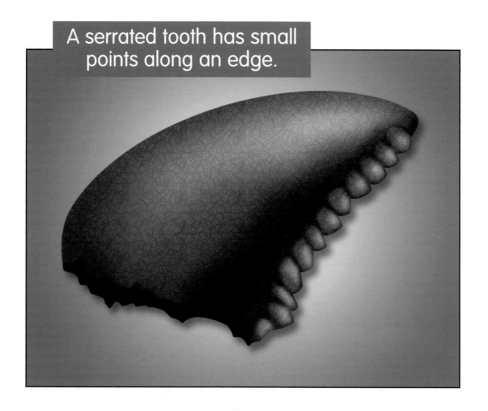
A serrated tooth has small points along an edge.

The Troodon was named after its deadly teeth. Troodon means "wounding tooth." This dinosaur's teeth were sharp and serrated. Serrated teeth have tiny, sharp points along an edge.

Some scientists believe the Troodon could see well in the dark. This skill would allow it to hunt animals at night. The Troodon probably ate anything it could catch and kill.

The Troodon may have hunted at night.

Many dinosaurs had an eye on each side of their head. These dinosaurs could not look forward like people do. The Troodon's eyes were set more on the front of its head. So, scientists believed it looked forward with both eyes. This would help the Troodon catch small, fast animals.

The Troodon may have lived near the Tyrannosaurus rex. This meat-eating dinosaur was much bigger than the Troodon. It stood about 18 feet (five m) tall. The Tyrannosaurus rex may have weighed about 10,000 pounds (4,536 kg). It was about 40 feet (12 m) long.

TYRANNOSAURUS REX

The Tyrannosaurus rex was about as long as a school bus.

Many scientists believe the Tyrannosaurus rex scavenged for food. Scavengers eat animals they did not kill. The Tyrannosaurus rex may have stolen food from other animals. Maybe it stole food from the Troodon.

The Tyrannosaurus rex may have scavenged for food.

21

THE FAMILY TREE

The Troodon belongs to the Troodontidae family. Troodontids had grabbing hands and large "killing claws." They had large eyes, too. Many scientists believe the Troodontids were the smartest dinosaurs.

Troodontid dinosaurs had large eyes.

23

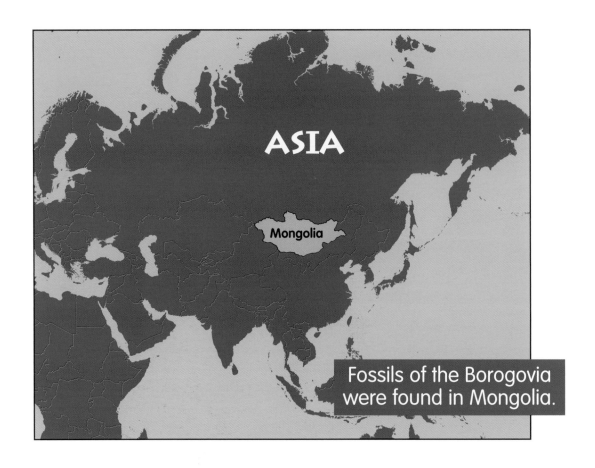

ASIA

Mongolia

Fossils of the Borogovia
were found in Mongolia.

Another Troodontid was the
Borogovia. It probably looked much
like the Troodon. The Borogovia lived
in what is now Mongolia.

DISCOVERY

Ferdinand V. Hayden found the first Troodon fossils in 1855. He found a Troodon tooth near the Judith River in Montana.

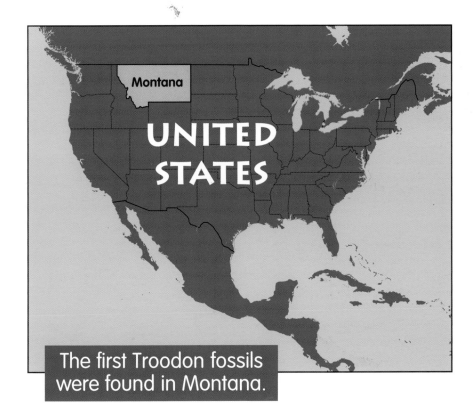

Montana

UNITED STATES

The first Troodon fossils were found in Montana.

Joseph Leidy was a paleontologist. He studied Hayden's Troodon tooth. Leidy did not believe the tooth belonged to a dinosaur. He thought the tooth belonged to a big lizard. Leidy named the Troodon in 1856.

Over the years, more Troodon bones were found. Many scientists studied these Troodon fossils. In the 1980s, scientists decided the Troodon was a dinosaur.

Fossils help people learn about dinosaurs.

American Museum of Natural History
Central Park West at 79th Street
New York, NY 10024-5192
http://www.amnh.org/

Museum of Paleontology
University of California
1101 Valley Life Sciences Building
Berkeley, CA 94720-4780
http://www.ucmp.berkeley.edu/

**Smithsonian National Museum
of Natural History**
10th Street and Constitution Avenue NW
Washington, D.C. 20560
http://www.nmnh.si.edu/paleo/index.html

Peabody Museum of Natural History
Yale University
170 Whitney Avenue
New Haven, CT 06520-8118
http://www.peabody.yale.edu/

TROODON

NAME MEANS	Wounding tooth
DIET	Meat
WEIGHT	100 pounds (45 kg)
LENGTH	7 feet (2 m)
TIME	Late Cretaceous Period
ANOTHER TROODONTID	Borogovia
SPECIAL FEATURE	Killing claw
FOSSILS FOUND	USA—Montana, Wyoming Canada—Alberta

The Troodon lived
75 million years ago.

The first humans appeared
1.6 million years ago.

Triassic Period	Jurassic Period	Cretaceous Period	Tertiary Period
245 Million years ago	208 Million years ago	144 Million years ago	65 Million years ago
	Mesozoic Era		Cenozoic Era

WEB SITES

To learn more about the Troodon, visit ABDO Publishing Company on the World Wide Web. Web sites about the Troodon are featured on our "Book Links" page. These links are routinely monitored and updated to provide the most current information available.

www.abdopub.com

carnivore a meat-eater.

Cretaceous period a period of time that happened 144–65 million years ago.

dinosaur a reptile that lived on land 248–65 million years ago.

fossil remains of very old animals and plants commonly found in the ground. A fossil can be a bone, a footprint, or any trace of life.

paleontologist someone who studies very old life, such as dinosaurs, mostly by studying fossils.

prey an animal that is food for other animals.

scavengers animals that eat animals they did not kill.

tropical weather that is warm and wet.

INDEX